WEALTH WISDOM

WEALTH WISDOM

JUDE HAWTHORNE

CONTENTS

1 Introduction to Wealth Wisdom   1
2 Historical Perspectives on Wealth   3
3 Modern Views on Money and Fulfillment   5
4 Psychological Aspects of Wealth   9
5 Cultural Influences on Wealth and Desire   13
6 Spiritual and Ethical Dimensions of Wealth   17
7 The Intersection of Wealth and Well-Being   21
8 Practical Strategies for Wealth Management   25
9 Personal Development and Wealth   29
10 Legacy Building and Wealth Transfer   33
11 Wealth Wisdom in the Digital Age   37
12 Conclusion: Embracing a Holistic Approach to Wealt   41

Copyright © 2024 by Jude Hawthorne
All rights reserved. No part of this book may be reproduced in any manner whatsoever without written permission except in the case of brief quotations embodied in critical articles and reviews.
First Printing, 2024

CHAPTER 1

Introduction to Wealth Wisdom

At times we can lose sight of the fact that human beings have been contemplating key elements of the human condition, such as wealth and wisdom, for thousands of years. In some cases, the world's great contemplative traditions have preserved a record of some of the best of this work, which was generated in response to the perennial human instincts to be prosperous and wise. Many insights into prosperity and knowledge have remained strong across the varying religious narratives and philosophical traditions through the millennia. This essay is devoted to exploring the multifaceted, deep well of wisdom in terms of these enduring human instincts and the traditions that still strive to refine them.

Prosperity involves more than acquiring money. Our desires, motivations, and beliefs about money influence us considerably. We must therefore appear to study how to address the mental, social, political, and spiritual hurdles effective preparedness for more sophisticated management of our property can present. Another interpretation of wealth wisdom might be known as wisdom wealth. From this perspective, prosperity from a bigger perspective - one that rests on the well-preserved pillars in which refined wealth wisdom is based - is what we lack. Wealth wisdom might help us look at the encouragement of ideals that do not have a price tag. It may help us recall the need to have lifestyles that guarantee more than just material safety. Wealth wisdom can surely help us facilitate the formation of a stumbling economy that does not seem right. And wealth wisdom would have incredible impetus to indicate a better understanding of what it means to be well-off.

Defining Wealth and Wisdom

What is wealth? What does it mean to be wise? Ideally, these questions - uttered and understood with new curiosity - will be revisited with fresh insight upon the completion of this essay. In our contemporary state of affairs, this pair of philosophic inquiries may strike some readers as peculiar or quaint. Even so, conversations concerning wealth, and wisdom - too often assumed to be antithetical - capture lasting interest, perhaps because we now know that neither can be legislated, bought, nor fully understood apart from the other. After all, we are all pioneering gaugers and plumbers of a sort.

Of course, the meaning of wealth - work, well-being, money, sociability - changes. Language and values fluctuate. The exchange of money and gifts, or an articulation of the human story, implicate moral philosophy. Moreover, wealth, its acquisition and proper use, is a subject of reflection extending from ancient India and Greece throughout the West and East to the present day. In this transaction of ideas, diverse voices offer enduring insights. Dao, a philosophy, is a "way": One might ask how one might live if one followed this way religiously. Wisdom, on the other hand, conveys "clear judgment, good sense." Hajime advises the apprentice, "Shlour. I give this to you."

CHAPTER 2

Historical Perspectives on Wealth

Nearly every book on wealth begins with a discussion of ancient origins. Wealth is, at its heart, an enduring hallmark of human endeavor, and how it is managed, spent, and thought about in our time is the fiery distillation of historical strivings, transgressions, and triumphs. Yet, do we really have much to learn from ancient texts on wealth? Yes, the wisdom of old rings loud and echoic in our present moment. Time cannot change human nature.

How we manipulate wealth has undergone massive transformation over the centuries, yet human conceptions of wealth have actually been less mutable. Furthermore, if the aim of the philosopher and theologian has been to examine the enduring myths of the human heart that bind each soul to the other, then wealth certainly deserves such a long and thoughtful examination. When are we too greedy, afraid, or charitable? When are we saved by a comfortable house? Enslaved by money changing hands? One historian poetically writes the answer to these two questions, "when, and how, one dies at the end of this life:" that their peace is ever on our minds guides our earthly decisions about wealth, making the wise old authors game guides on a tour through our own monetary attitudes.

Ancient Philosophies and Wealth

The association of wealth with enduring aspirations beyond the satisfaction of material comforts is also a resonant theme in ancient Hellenistic philosophies of Epicureanism, Stoicism, Pyrrhonism, Platonism, and Aristotelianism. Historically, these ancient philosophical attitudes towards wealth and poverty have been trivialized within present scholarly disciplines of economics, philosophy, and psychology because wealth has commonly been seen as a peripheral preoccupation in the moral philosophies of these bygone eras. The principal insight of this essay is that when these ancient sensibilities and doctrines are viewed broadly through the lenses of ethics, spiritual philosophy, and the practical wisdom of living a good human life, then we see that careful listeners will discern in these ancient philosophies both an abiding reluctance to attain economic wealth per se and distinct ways to construe the functions and effects of wealth as such whose moral import is still comprehensible today.

The term 'wealth' bears historical associations with everything from profane opulence to heavenly treasure, and with the ambiguous blessings of poverty and simplicity or need and deprivation. Some Christian doctrines still echoing Platonic philosophy, for example, enjoin asceticism, voluntary poverty, charity, and substance intolerance in whose practice we find a persistent concern with or ambivalence about the deleterious effects of wealth both for the rich and the poor. The perennial power and appeal of these traditions suggest that there may be something of broad interest and continuing import in the prejudices of times of yore about wealth. From these talking points our first aim in this essay will be to indicate in tension with prevailing dogmas a variety of ancient Hellenistic perspectives and teachings on wealth across different interpretive traditions.

CHAPTER 3

Modern Views on Money and Fulfillment

Today, tremendous attention surrounds wealth and its material fruits. From BusinessWeek to the Bulls, Fortune to Forbes, the Wall Street Journal to CNBC, scarcely a publication or broadcast is indifferent. To be sure, the magnitude and multiplication of wealth in recent times rivet attention. Yet fascination with wealth—and its accoutrements—goes beyond dollars and denominations. Our subject is what we (don't) do for the money, which gets us into the realm of money and fulfillment.

On the one hand, the inveterate critic may make money the barometer of panting, value-swerving soullessness. On the other hand, the dyed-in-the-wool entrepreneur (of which there are many lately) or capitalist may harbor neither doubt nor hesitation about the salubrious ascent to fulfillment taken via ample lucre. And, on the third hand, and even though they might be incapable of saying as much, these savvy souls of curves and threads commensurate with those of bound and duty. The line between duty and carryings-forth is too faint to make out in matters of life.

These days, a somewhat different version of wealth and fulfillment manifests. Not in the mood of those listed above, but rather as an illustration of modern attitudes toward muckmucks and personal attainment, this "modern views" segues to modern ideas about feeling and action, want and satisfaction (in three steps). Comparable to earlier times, the topic of cash, what it brings, and whether it can or has been put to right ends aside from its exchange on the ground is one still inflaming discussion.

In the 21st century, many are agog about (although often attitudinally stuck with) how serial pleasurable moments are supposed to get them going where they regard themselves as wanting to go. Instead of the town of doing-as-such and the contentious landscape of achievement, here the topic is desire, want, immaterial fulfillment, the practical cool.

Economic Theories and Happiness

Economic theories of the relation between wealth and happiness cover a spectrum. On one end lie the theories proposing that they are irredeemably opposed. These theories argue that income inequality (and acquiring wealth more generally) is the seedbed of social decay and corruption, producing greed in some people and dissatisfaction and resentment in the rest. In the modern terms of market-economy capitalism, the zero-sum theorists argue that our competitive marketplace habituates us to believe that our fellow human beings are obstacles to our desire for well-being rather than potential collaborators in its pursuit, to use Honore de Balzac's formulation. This response to despairing atomism is an essential theme for critics of contemporary market society.

These theories of the dark side of wealth hold that the economy either reflects or metaphorically embodies the desires of its participants, desires that are expressed in measurable quantities. Furthermore, they hold that if the participants require more and more to be satisfied, it is evident that they are not, in fact, satisfied, regardless of the fact that they will claim that they are. The evidence of the discontent of demand can be confirmed by the increasingly large quantities of goods and services that society requires to produce to satisfy that demand. Crude, this is and remains, the rhetorical question: "Just how many Rolexes and Hermes scarves can you wear?".

CHAPTER 4

Psychological Aspects of Wealth

The motivations behind acquiring wealth rest in the intricacies of a wanting mind. To address the multifaceted roles these assets play in providing a fulfilled life, we will consider the inner self who sees the mind's confusion. Discovering a deeper psychological nature will inform our external self and shine light on why we may find our thinking, emotions, and behaviors so challenging. From an evolutionary perspective, the human mind excelled at promoting our continued existence through adaptations that led to survival alongside the social environment. Applied to wealth, our minds encouraged asset accumulation because, at an elemental level, possessing liquid investments allowed us to continue to "buy" life's assets, from physiological needs like food to self-actualized aspects.

Psychological research establishes that whether a person's pursuits are the desire for power (achieved through money/wealth), the pursuit of extrinsic vs. intrinsic goals, ascending the corporate hierarchy, or taking on more financial risk, "gobs and gobs" of money do not bring about fulfillment. Research suggests happiness improves with income at lower amounts. Cognitive dissonance theory states that rationalization follows a decision, which we see with income hoarding when it is already within an individual's value structure or when someone tells a wealth manager that they want to make as much money as possible. We now have evidence suggesting psychological dimensions play a direct role in the acquisition and management of money, beliefs about whether individual behaviors will cover consumption shortfalls, and individual desires to maintain more wealth in order to assuage insecurity. We can begin unraveling individual motives behind wealth management and uncover what role psychological dynamics play in wealth outcomes.

The Psychology of Wealth Acquisition

The fact that much more performance feedback is given to men than to women may deter firms from experimenting with putting more women in line positions. If the psychological point of view is correct, having different methods of financing the two programs will drive a wedge between the attractiveness of the two programs and, in the authors' basic model, make the decentralized firm indifferent between them.

The financial and economic sciences prize is given to Robert Shiller and Lawrence Summers for creatively and effectively integrating finance, microeconomics, and behavioral psychology into modern empirical research on investment and saving over time by default when charges are waived by customer companies for other services bought by the transport customer. The Huttig shareholders approved the merger in this segment last month. The rail merger, expected at the end of this year, is subject to other customary regulatory approvals.

Investment by an individual is an ultimate result of philanthropic and economic factors. Together, these factors discredit communications from practitioners and consultants to investors. Firms assigning special accounts to experts providing poorly performing advisors develop the credibility of the account for the expert, taking into account the weak performance of the company. Investors risk confusing luck with expertise; however, overconfidence may explain gambling in casinos. As the probability of wild casino gambling falls, the Ku is likely to fall as investors do not become overconfident. Purists claim that gambling is irrational.

CHAPTER 5

Cultural Influences on Wealth and Desire

Wealth, desire, and the term "good life" have impacted the world both morally and spiritually. Whole cultures have based rituals or daily activities around notions of what constitutes a comfortable life and good personal value and purpose. This want for what we call rich culture can be very hard to determine through any amount of research. Often, feelings related to these deep-rooted and non-conscious aspects of one's self will change with each generation. Our attitudes about wealth are shaped by generations of intentional and oftentimes hidden cultural indoctrination. Culture can be thought of as a "tool kit" that dispenses shared meanings, values, behaviors, and traditions, carrying individuals as they travel through life, from life stage to life stage. People working in fields as disparate as agriculture, psychology, sociology, and economics have long noted that there is a complex and continually evolving balance between individual predilections and collective tastes. Here, we use the term "values" to describe the intentionally shared meanings, beliefs, and assumptions that fuel wealthy cultures.

The interaction between rich people and poor folk is deeply culturally embedded. Deeper than even English common laws of property and the development of formal markets lies the development of time-honored family rituals, values, and traditions. The embeddedness of wealthy interactions resisted change through colonialism, modernization, and even urbanization. Therefore, one's day-to-day culture-based attitude can seem to revolve around daily rituals and a physical standard of living. A wealthy culture holds beliefs about what is "good" and "valuable," beautiful, or "luxurious" that will change as members in a good life culture grow and adapt. Sub-cultures within this group with distinctive lifestyles tend to shape this broader understanding of value. Sub-cultures can grow even more distinct over generations, resulting in varying attraction to newer desires, including "new money" desires.

Consumerism and Materialism

Sentinel on January 31, 2022, entitled "Wealth Wisdom". Published for the Young Writers Scholarship, this essay received a perfect score and guaranteed a junior in high school an opportunity to attend a week-long Iowa Young Writers' Studio in summer 2023! Published online and in print, the article managed to magically rank in the top five most-read articles on the "Sentinel" website for the week as well.

Our culture swims in consumerism. Reducing desire for material things may provide some relief, but consider also examining our materialism. Consumerism is each generation shopping from catalogs different than the last, each dissatisfied with the old stuff while continuing to pile up new stuff, all the while insisting that platonic satisfaction is just a few Teslas and Powerball jackpots out of reach.

At first glance, we may suspect that consumer culture began with a conspiracy in the last century. Salesmen took off their vinyl mustaches and gathered in corporate undercroft to plan an information campaign. They said, "Come children, indulge your desires with ease; just sign here and promise to pay me later - with lots of interest!" But the scarcity mentality of consumers did not spring from some top-secret marketing blueprint, but rather is a response to a time and place. Coming of age in a place as wealthy and sprawling as West Michigan, we can be tempted to take such material surplus for granted. The materialism-connected set of perspectives about the inherently unsatisfactory qualities of wealth and the inward turning necessary for fulfillment have become like society's air, something to analyze once in shortage. Wealth does indeed stand in the way of desire, but like a mirror.

CHAPTER 6

Spiritual and Ethical Dimensions of Wealth

Despite its clear religious and moral dimensions, wealth also has a spiritual resonance. Spirituality is broader than religion. It concerns the drive to live a fuller, more expansive life—in the sense of transcending ourselves coupled with our desire for a deep sense of connection to transcendent values and realities. Wealth is a means to this more expansive life.

At the same time, tradition also presents ethical cautions about wealth, particularly the lack of character that can emerge with wealth secured easily and quickly. One key issue concerns the ways wealth impinges on our integration as human beings. Wealth can call us into a more integrated life by enabling us to do what we truly love, but this is true to the extent that we are not subject to the corrosive effects of unchecked acquisitiveness. Beyond the generation of income-wealth, another question posed by personal choice of vocation is this: What values or meanings rise to the level that we will be willing to sacrifice the possibility of using our God-given gifts in another field in order to remain true to our values? There is a strong spiritual and ethical resonance to this reverberating question.

The topic of "wealth" at least engages two or more elements: a description or reality element, and an evaluative or normative dimension. This evaluative or normative dimension of wealth is the primary focus of this essay. Descriptively understood, wealth pertains to valued goods or persons, and includes "specimen wealth" or goods of personal value, e.g., providing a person with food, shelter, clothing, and other forms of economic security, as well as the beauty of art and the good of friendship, and "ordered wealth" or goods and distributions of goods that are beneficial to common existence, such as community goods like justice, education, and universal access to goods.

Religious Teachings on Wealth

In our modern, contemporary world, cutting-edge research and technological advances have brought us many new insights and understandings of various kinds. A formidable array of business, economics, finance, and social science theories hold our attention and stimulate our curiosity. For some communities of people, however, both now and throughout history, religion—its ancient texts, rituals, stories, beliefs, and values—remains the bedrock upon which they make sense of the world in its sacred, profane, and mundane dimensions. Rather than constricting rationality, religious traditions seek to shape and guide our lives in the ordinary moments that sustain us, lifting us out of ourselves toward a richer understanding of who we are, how we are to relate to one another, and ultimately, stand in relation to God or the transcendent.

Our lives are a part of an intricate, ever-changing shalom, kosmos, salaam, or world: whatever name one gives it, these traditions see the acquisition and use of wealth as a profound and deeply ethical exercise. In other words, religious traditions do not generally concern themselves with the accumulation of wealth as a matter of financial gain or on account of material security or acquisition; rather, the acquisition and disposition of wealth is a spiritual or theological matter with important ethical implications for the kind of communities and individuals we are called to be. While each of these traditions has within it an array of beliefs and interpretive communities, the religious teachings that follow offer the community of business a profound and ancient reflection on ethics, money, and the purposes to which wealth is directed and employed. The various religious traditions we will consult offer not a secular, but a spiritual or theological understanding of wealth that can significantly inform contemporary business practice, contextualizing the socio-economic effects of such practical wisdom that emanates not only from the world of finance or of moral theory, but from an abiding sense of our shared and ultimate purpose in the world fashioned by the Divine.

CHAPTER 7

The Intersection of Wealth and Well-Being

While for many, wealth is its own reward, there is also significant interest in assessing the extent to which wealth can positively influence other facets of an individual's well-being—assuming one subscribes to hedonic adaptation, the Easterlin paradox, and the other aforementioned theoretical crossroads. The financial benefits of being wealthier are widespread and multifarious. There are many benefits to being rich, relative to being poor or even merely comfortable. Some emotional benefits can be bought, while others might be a function of socioeconomic status. Empirically, being richer is associated with greater subjective well-being (SWB), emotional well-being, marital satisfaction, and mental health up to a threshold somewhere between $100,000 and $200,000 a year. It is also negatively associated with, and even predicts future reductions in, perceived stress and physical morbidities such as heart disease, stroke, diabetes, hypertension, arthritis, and a range of other chronic diseases. Wealth not only impacts individual well-being but also economically, physically, and psychologically influences overall well-being. It is our hope that others might find some use in acquainting themselves with the following pieces of wisdom—systematically collected from history and other diverse sources—through which individuals, societies, and economic actors across all walks of life have and continue to strive to achieve positive well-being through a meaningful blend of individual and collective wealth maximization and fulfillment-based value systems.

It turns out that wealth, broadly construed, is associated with a surprising array of actual—and potential—positive externalities. In particular, the relationships in this domain seem to be tripartite: (1) Greater wealth tends to afford individuals with the knowledge, training, leisure, or financial resources to allocate more attention and resources to things like mental health, social connections, and knowledge accumulation; (2) These various intermediate ends are often separate determinants of, or are correlated with, measures of subjective well-being; and (3) Increases in these varied intermediate ends generally lead to direct or durable increases in meaningful markers of individual and even collective well-being. It's important to thread our way through the additional potential theoretical snags, albeit specific to the domain of individual and collective well-being, that have emerged in the relatively nascent interdisciplinary subfield of "happiness economics" in order to reach the heart of our well-being-and-wealth inquiry. Two accessory elements of the well-being-wealth dynamic may have the capacity to complicate our chronological and interdisciplinary trek. First, there are indications that there may exist an informal area of disagreement bordering on contradiction in the literature surrounding well-being and wealth. Second, establishing and maintaining high levels of well-being is very complex. There are so many interacting parts of a person's well-being that the encouraging or damaging effects of a $50,000 pay cut or bonus very often become imperceptible within one full year or less.

Health and Wealth

We spend a great deal of time earning money, investing money, spending money, and even worrying about money. All such activities seem to assume that a main objective of life is to become financially secure or wealthy. Many people behave as if money, or the things it can buy, is so deeply connected to happiness that a significant increase oftentimes seems to produce a substantial boost in overall joy. In surveys about what individuals plan to achieve in life, large percentages indicate that what they really want from life is not all that much money; instead, they hope to be earning the amount of money they have targeted for achievement in a job that they love.

There are far-ranging relationships of wealth to health, or the absence of it. Individual financial circumstances play a major role in how healthy you are. Wealthier Americans tend to have better access to quality healthcare, are more likely to make lifestyle choices such as diet, smoking, and seatbelt use that improve bodily functioning, and possess better mental health. The access to these resources can be limited if resources were allocated solely based on subjective needs. For those with high incomes, they can afford better information on healthcare, better access, and either complete sidedness in choice or outright control of the care they receive. For those with lower incomes, in many forms of universal insurance coverage, these same factors cannot be had in such quantities. Consequently, better healthcare can be had on better sides of extensive waiting lists, vastly offset by better income-paying ability.

CHAPTER 8

Practical Strategies for Wealth Management

From common folk on a budget to grand emperors dreaming of lasting empires, everyone wants wealth that lasts. Wealth preservation is part of wealth management, but we also require a positive rate of return and need to grow our wealth. Here comes reinvesting capital gains into new spreading of capital, compounding over multiple years! Many of you know that along with long-term investing, the tenets of compounding are the bedrock of wealth.

From the above investment wisdom, we can derive a few practical rules for wealth preservation and wealth management: Be wary of 'into-this-and-out-of-that-strategy; invest with a clear, well-thought-out, long-term plan that specifies the assets you are going to buy (equities, debt funds, etc.). Rebalance between assets judiciously. Invest in assets whose returns beat the inflation rate. The only asset for which you need not rebalance is the Risk-Free Portfolio (we will discuss this a bit later). Hold some cash in reserve to be able to take advantage of opportunities if assets crash. Never look at your portfolio balance each day or even monthly because you may be tempted to act impulsively. Great investments are like fine wines, they need time to appreciate - so don't watch its price daily. When your emotional wounds prevent you from sticking to all the above rules, take help from a financial planner or a behavioral finance coach - good financial advisors help you balance emotion and analysis. Entrepreneurs: Equity investments in India have long-term advantages, are investing in growing small-medium-size enterprises. You are investing in companies. The above strategies make common (and financial) sense - but most investors do not follow them. The reasons for this are formidable: human mind and emotions. So I give up - and the industry gives fund management results. For a good money manager to some extent highly probable, for an outstanding-to-impossible.

From Common Folk to Emperors, everyone wants wealth that lasts. Wealth preservation is part of wealth management, but we also require a positive rate of return and need to grow our wealth. Here comes reinvesting capital gains into new spreading of capital, compounding over multiple years. Great investments are like fine wines, they need time to appreciate - so don't watch its price daily. When your emotional wounds prevent you from sticking to an investment plan, take help from a financial planner or a behavioral finance coach - good financial advisors help you balance emotion and analysis. "There is little merit in a technique that gets you in, but no rules for when to get out. Every successful investment involves getting into the markets at the right time just as surely as it brings composure when the prices fall. Patience means enduring foolishness long enough for the market to rebalance values back to realistic levels. Of course, some business ideas will prove to be too costly when implemented over time. But the biggest loss of all is the reduced result that comes from trying to avoid all losses." 'Egan: Fundamental Analysis Of Stock Company'

Investment Principles

There are no "can't-miss" investment strategies for consistently producing high returns with low risk. However, on a general basis, wise investing shares several key attributes, including the following:

- All investments are subject to greater, lesser, or a combination of the risks of capital loss, time-cost, and purchasing power erosion. Rate of return over the long haul is primarily commensurate with the degree of risk of the investment.

- Investments are frequently associated with higher risks. While the potential long-term prospects can be greater in emerging industries or markets, it is seldom realistic to expect high reward without a commensurate level of risk.

- Volatility principle: In the short run, the price of all securities fluctuates widely, often denying orderly market behavior. The combining of risk, reward, and time is at the heart of all investment decision-making. The three are inseparable. If one, for example, could obtain relatively high reward with low risk in a very short time, the process of accumulating and increasing wealth would take on a different rationale. Withdrawn from theoretical and formulaic issues to specific everyday living, the risk versus return versus time principle makes either inherently "right" or "wrong" investment choices, at best, less clear. Misguided, however, can be the pursuit of the value, either real or illusory, that can inhere in the investment marketplace, drawing attention from an investment's ability to meet one's particular lifestyle objectives.

CHAPTER 9

Personal Development and Wealth

It's both fluffy and profound, irksome and delightful: the deep and sometimes enragingly obvious assumption that your character is directly connected to your wealth. That is, after all, the implication of any time spent on you book - that you are not only dissatisfied with your moolah, but that the truth about how to get more has to do with your attitude, emotions, approach, vision, strengths, resilience, choices, (un)willingness to ask, and who you are willing to piss off. Consumer North America and its British dominion is rife with people who want to preach this nonsense - take Tony Robbins, please.

Truth be told, the case that there is a link between fortune and fortitude is not entirely baseless. Call it resilience. Beyond "sucking it up" is the truth. You need cash to grow your number one asset: you. The risk for entrepreneurs and such is, clever planners, to assume that you need cash in order to grow. In a narrow sense, yes. But Cash-in-your-hand-itis is also a prescription for learned helplessness. Viscerally spooked to realize all you have to work with is you, your resilience blossoms. Can you do it again? Given other profitable alternatives, you are far less likely to tolerate caffeinated mini-marshmallow-induced emergencies. Wouldn't it be romantic to have enough dash to provide a financial womb in which to gestate your business baby? But, says the book, that is not development. And development is the point.

Mindset Shifts for Financial Success

The last couple of decades have seen a significant shift in mentality when it comes to money and wealth. The current popular philosophy and mindset reflects an entitlement mentality – the idea that "we don't have to wait for it - we deserve it now." The desire for instant gratification is markedly different from the frugality associated with the WWII generation and the transmutation and psycho-spiritual aspects of the laws of success. A powerful individual doesn't go chasing money - instead, they attract wealth regardless of their present circumstances.

We often notice a sense of despair and a defeatist mentality in some clients we meet who feel overwhelmed by the complexity and depth of the psychology and societal impact issues surrounding wealth creation. That's what I refer to as the "Martian effect" - the mental concepts and strategies developed and utilized by wealthy individuals are diametrically alien to the average Australian's modus operandi or mental programming. Several successful private clients have made a fascinating shift from despair to empowerment after the realization that they don't have to believe in 5000 Martian concepts to be empowered around wealth. These concepts of psychic empowerment and phenomenological enfranchisement have the net effect of enhancing both personal growth and empowerment far beyond the goods and services purchased by their wealth. If wealth is no longer an unobtanium and better experienced now, the reason for its pursuit necessarily changes from just the narcissism of having a large bank account. Initiating this in action has a feedback effect of salience - more opportunities for growth, empowerment, and wealth are noticed and flourish in that mindset, while evidence for existing in a zero-sum, greedy alienated existence is reframed as counterproductive and unprofitable, done by losers and enemies.

CHAPTER 10

Legacy Building and Wealth Transfer

Legacy and estate planning invite a natural contemplation on wealth transfer and the dynamics associated with who will be good stewards of family assets - or, at the least, not squander them. While important, we believe that this viewpoint is too narrow. For insights on wealth transfer and its human dimensions to be of enduring interest, we must leverage them to shine a light on legacy. For its proponents, legacy is about much more than money. "An inheritance is the money you leave behind to your family. Your legacy is the values, stories, and experiences your family takes forward as a result of what you leave them." But, an inside job this is not. Despite how creative people tend to get when saving as "wealth artists," as he puts it, envisioning legacy suddenly becomes difficult. And when the question turns to how a uniqueness-inspired "keeper of the castle" transfers it, sentences become shorter, stuttering commences, and "Erm, um, I don't really know..." often fall off the tongue. Just 22 months of this meant "the third generation spent what the second generation saved" and left no trust for them to rest on. Legacy matters.

Many of the panels, podcasts, and papers at this sixth annual symposium on wealth are dedicated to tax-efficient wealth transfer: from one's deathbed to the next generation. But, remind the authors of "Wealth," making a mark beyond oneself - sans tax - is a continuous task in wealth holders' gift-giving strategies. This essay marshals the advice of substance and streets to help scholars and professionals alike understand how to do this masterfully. Should legacy be confused with property and life insurance (important as these areas are)? No, though the distinction between (financial) and legacy building is seldom in the literature. Yoga wisdom conveys that to-dough it was an ancient cash-driven custom to cover the dead - the act of bequeathing lightens the heart. Often personally, legacy begetting (versus financial planning for death) helps wills join generations rather than "divide the house." Costales signs off an interview when the dying man's message stops being "What will happen upon my death?" and begins to say, "After I'm gone, what will continue?" or "How do I carry on?"

Estate Planning

Estate planning is the process of managing and/or transferring personal holdings, large or small, during a lifetime or upon death, through methods and structures created by individual states and jurisdictions, while attempting to provide for efficient administration and protection of the assets against litigation, unnecessary taxes, and overreaching claimants. The creation of instruments notwithstanding, estate planning is most properly viewed as a cooperative effort between individuals and their chosen accountants, attorneys, and financial advisors to arrange for orderly transfer of wealth between living adult human beings, dying human beings, and human beings who are long dead. To that end, this presentation will address in order certain core topics that interlink the essential considerations of legal and fiscal realm with money, desire, and human nature itself. These topics include: the construction of human values (Why Bother?), the principles and basic organization of estate planning, and the strategies which may be pursued in order to minimize the risk of necessary redress.

At its core, estate planning is concerned with the orderly transfer of assets from one generation to another, as directed by the givers according to a certain order and range of preferences. The study and practice of estate planning are something like a sociology of the dead. It is through the structures and strictures of estates that the living receive the residue of the loves of the dead. While it is true that estate planning is a branch of the general field of "will-making," it will be helpful in our examination to consider the field independent from the narrow significance given to the term in law. Like the tree botanist who studies anatomy while his colleague concentrates on system, so at times we will prefer a species to a genus perspective. In the former context the laws of the property estate in America, as it has evolved in several jurisdictions since the inception of the 20th century, will be critically evaluated. Such an approach uses the laws of the tax estate as data, and is not strictly a matter of legal research. To complete our examination, we will attempt to synthesize the material and look to generally acceptable and human considerations in the planning and management of individual estates. For the person likely to face estate tax, especially from those states refusing to allow the benefits of federal credits, the creation of a sharing trust, or a bypass or survivor trust (terms often used by tax attorneys) may be essential to safeguard vested interests in wealth.

CHAPTER 11

Wealth Wisdom in the Digital Age

Wealth Wisdom, the theme of Garden Talks 2016, is the title of Atul K. Shah's collection of disparate reflections from various professionals and thought leaders, including himself. This book, now in its second edition, is obviously a timely exploration of financial life, and its subtitle reveals further insights. Wealth Wisdom: Enduring Insights on Money, Desire, and Fulfillment connects the theme of money and wealth with desire and fulfillment, only then doing the work virtually every other essay we have actually emphasized: the elucidation of relationships between the economy (finance, in our case) and the broader cultural, even religious, values informing human existence.

The allure of the title and subtitle is the appeal to 'enduring insights'. This essay is an inquiry into the meaning and significance of the title and subtitle of Shah's collection in the context of global digital culture, considering how digital wealth wisdom may open up new ethical and cultural possibilities. A competitive edge is best understood in the frame of technological advancement. While technologically human-centric wisdom traditions offer tools for harnessing the ethical potential of the digital in ways that meet contemporary socio-economic demands, they also help us to critique such demands, exposing the depths of institutionalized digital poverty. Market low wealth accumulation, myopic shareholder value, the degradation of democratic institutions, and moral exit strategies compound digital wealth wisdom's tension between the ancient and emerging market. Market optimism thrives as financial and technological innovation merge, giving rise to new profit-making opportunities. Web 3.0 companies continue to explore fragmenting financial space. In doing so, they challenge institutional traditions ingeniously engineered throughout the past 200 years to benefit the elite. The greatest threat Bitcoin poses is both a regulatory and institutional one. The digital age is sprawling with opportunities to provide financial services to a host of people the market, illegitimately, has rendered unworthy of the advisement, protection, and support of legitimate finance. The not-so-distant Third World / First World split has not given way, even though we are living in the digital age. So in what ways are the wealth wisdom of Atul K. Shah and digital technology consistent or compatible, and in what ways are they contradictory? Digital wealth wisdom does not solve this conundrum but provides approaches to its analysis.

Fintech Innovations

Fintech is one of the fastest-growing sectors of the world's digital transformation. The sector shares the insights of digital transformation while focusing on disruptions in wealth management services and financial advice, as well as in new ventures in innovative insurance services. Banks traditionally offer wealth management services for their most affluent clients, providing asset management, investment advice, estate planning, tax optimization, and legal assistance, including advice in case of divorce. Experts have to be hired or acquired to offer these individualized services, which require legal investment advice and trading. Digital platforms are developing to offer greater opportunities through a range of investments and financial products while extending these services to clients with any wealth level. Part of the objective is to broaden the clients' portfolio with low-cost retail investments, so the focus on the wealthy clients has irritated the market.

The distributed ledger technology, also known as blockchain, aims to open a range of services in different industries since its inception. In wealth management services, this technology aims to encourage people to invest in highly illiquid investments such as real estate. In addition, developments in technology ventures have become new banks, the neobanks, targeting the needs and pain points of high-net-worth clients, and insurances with loss prevention technologies. Wealth management services and financial advice have stood the test of time. They are suitable for all ages, cultures, assets, and nationalities. Nevertheless, the growth of new technologies aims to financially empower the bulk of people by dispersing opportunities for investment and offering insurance for property in highly industrialized regions, where floods destroying homes and property are an increasing threat.

CHAPTER 12

Conclusion: Embracing a Holistic Approach to Wealt

In conclusion, the universal truth of holism will not be denied. In this book, you've heard from me and from 33 very wise people in a wide variety of traditions. You may have found some ideas foreign and surprising, or you may have found wisdom that inspired you.

You've heard about money, desire, and fulfillment that bring lasting and unwavering joy. You've heard about how to be helpful and take care of yourself. You've heard how to think, how to make wise and prudent decisions, how to prioritize, and how to know what's enough. You know what anxiety about your estate might be doing provocatively to other people, and what other people's reaction to your estate might be doing to you. You've heard about the underlying forces that shape our desires and about finding your own purpose as an individual. You've heard enough to know that wealth is not just about money, nor is it just about what you think, nor is it just about what we think as individuals, nor is it just about what we think within our corporate boundaries. But wealth is about the confluence of money, psychology, and ethics—and wealth is, ultimately, a social and ethical issue. Our intentions are perhaps set for greater engagement, and our time has now been well spent. We will be left with two main messages. First, wisdom traditions across the ages unanimously proclaim the holistic dimension of wealth. Second, our contemporary AWM agent (that would be you, the reader...) needs more than just a good asset allocation and a will in order to reach his life goals and to "have enough." If we as a field had any reflective capacity at all, the current confusion and seeming alienation of AWM practitioners would be enough to cause us to step back and aside and re-evaluate our theoretical and practical convictions. Our best hope is that something in this volume creates a sympathetic vibration in your heart: that in broadening your perspectives, you come to feel a stronger sense of just possible it is to bring more integrity into your work.

www.ingramcontent.com/pod-product-compliance
Lightning Source LLC
LaVergne TN
LVHW092101060526
838201LV00047B/1498